A FEELING
CALLED HEAVEN

A FEELING CALLED HEAVEN

JOEY YEAROUS-ALGOZIN

NIGHTBOAT BOOKS
NEW YORK

Copyright © 2021 by Joey Yearous-Algozin
Printed in the United States

ISBN: 978-1-64362-077-0
Design and Typesetting by NOR Research Studio
Text set in New Spirit and Times New Roman

Cataloging-in-publication data is available from
the Library of Congress

Nightboat Books
New York
www.nightboat.org

A generation goes, and a generation comes, but the earth remains forever. — *Ecclesiastes* 1:3

The ignorance and loathing for this new thing that would be and would come presently were terrible; yet he said that nothing was more oppressive for him at that moment than the constant thought: 'What if I were not to die! What if life were given back to me—what infinity! And it would all be mine! Then I'd turn each minute into a whole age, I'd lose nothing, I'd reckon up every minute separately, I'd let nothing be wasted!' He said that in the end this thought turned into such anger in him that he wished they would hurry up and shoot him. — Fyodor Dostoevsky, *The Idiot*

for the second to last time

I wanted to show you something

that would give you pleasure

before the end of the world

I thought I would play you a video of antelope or deer

moving as a herd across an expanse of green grass

shot from the door of a helicopter

flying in unison with the animals below

as the repurposed foundation

for the death of this planet in X number of years

for there's nothing to be done now

but love

and embrace the silence

of our impending destruction as a species

offered the gift of consciousness

through accident or divine fiat

that has done little with it

but slightly lessen the suffering

of a few

i.e. the bar was so low and desire so brutal

there's nothing to be done now

but to await our own destruction

in the presence of each other

this patience then is really all that's necessary

not saying how the world could be better

it can't be better

a better world isn't possible

but patience is possible

meditation on a few moments of intense deprivation

on all that's left

this impoverishment we've been given

ecstatic reduction

or a feeling called heaven

that speaks to itself

of nothing but a final annihilation

that arrives quietly

though it remains perhaps forever in the distance

I wanted to show you something

that would remind you of a time in your life

before we came together

as a way of finding some trace

of pleasure or happiness

in the presence of each other

this is not a rejection of the world

but a radical acceptance of our own impoverishment

that allows us to welcome passivity

as a way of reducing both the mind and body

to the minimal frequency necessary

to maintain this place we now occupy together

as we wait for the true end of the world

which is already here

and yet

has only just begun

an end

that began without us

but because of us

and now

no longer needs us

as it makes its way

slowly

through each and every one of us

and each and every successive generation

I want you to allow this feeling called heaven

which is little more than a recognition of our presence

here

together

an acknowledgement that we're not outside the world

and yet

nothing's demanded of us

to create a modicum

of calm and stability

sitting here

in the company of each other

because the world is dying

(at least for us)

we've made it an inhospitable place for us

and yet there's pleasure to be found

in the beginning of the end of the world

as you sit listening

to my voice speaking to you

I want you to remember

that this is only the beginning of the end

and so we're embarking on this journey together

or more accurately

we're engaged in a process of reduction

that erases any distinction

between you and anyone else

so that you become just one body among many

a material object severed from its utility

merely occupying this space for a time

in this way we come to regard

this wretched thing we call our body

this vessel or vehicle

as little more than a seat of pain and frustration

yet one we hold so dear

as it shrinks in terror at night

as the room in which you're lying down or sitting up

listening to the sound of my voice

settles around you

with a noise

disconnected from any discernible source

which for that brief moment

makes you all too aware of your own fragility

or at other times

as it swells with anxiety

something you feel welling within you

say

on the train

when the arm of a stranger sitting next to you

relaxes against your side

gently pressing into your ribs

as you resist the urge to turn your face

and look at this person sitting next to you

to acknowledge this physical closeness

and inadvertent touch

that wants nothing from you but needs a place to rest

a place at the beginning of the end

that we cannot see

but rest assured

for this moment together

in the calmness of its late arrival

and in this way you can think of my words

what I have to say to you

as constructing something like a side altar

a place for us

to watch for those who'll eventually come and replace us

only to keep this watch in our place

for we're little more than surrogates

who've come to regard this vessel or vehicle

this wretched thing we call our body

as something like a coat or sweater

placed gently on the chair beside you

in a darkened movie theater

holding this place beside you

for a friend who is on their way to meet you

but has been delayed

and whose absence

gives you a reason to keep sitting where you are

and as such we come to occupy this space

between what came before

and an end that has already arrived

visualized in this way

we can understand this beginning

as it occurs in the distance

far from us

as something like a boundary

or more accurately a wall

to gently lean against

as we sit together

here

in each other's company

I ask that you focus

not on the individual thoughts

as they pass through your mind

but on the structure of your mind

as the channel that these thoughts travel through

as the unconscious

communicates with the conscious mind

giving meaning to all your interactions with the world

your beliefs and habits

your feelings and emotions

each individual sensation is simply

a message

or information

traveling through the very material

by which you've come to understand

say

the trauma you underwent in being

expelled from your mother's body

of gradually assuming

this separate and isolated character

the faint noise

in the background of your mind

as you close your eyes

and listen to the sound of my voice

as my voice and your own thoughts become one

and move together

from the foreground to the background

fading into a dull hum of atmospheric static

not unlike the hum of the air conditioner

that keeps the room you're sitting in

at a comfortable 70 degrees

allow your attention to wander away from my voice

and listen to these ambient sounds

that vie for your attention daily

these parallel tracks coming together in the mind

to create the hushed sound of traffic

in the street below your window

or your upstairs neighbor

moving a chair

against the hardwood floor of their living room

and as you listen to these layers of sound

I want you to remember that this hum

is the sound of our collective death

which we patiently embrace

even if unconsciously

accepting this knowledge

that emerges as the foundation of our lives together

not only will we perish individually

but our time as a species is drawing to a close

and while this knowledge remains unthinkable

there are moments

here

together

where we can envision the quiet that would exist

without us

the clouds break

and the sun glints off pools of irradiated water

outside a freeway on-ramp

or hospital parking lot

in which a few discarded syringes

and fragments of plastic tubing

bob in the light breeze

traveling across a world

emptied of our presence

I want you to hold

in your mind

this image of a future world continuing without us

arising

from a communal hope

that once we've disappeared

this world will reach a quiet equilibrium

the weather again becoming pleasant

the wind no longer carrying the scent of rotting garbage

or chemicals

burning in the chimney of an anonymous factory

the sweet smell bringing solidity

as if the seemingly endless supply of gummy plastic

burning somewhere beyond the factory's walls

had reconstituted in your lungs

such that now you carry it with you

in a minor way

and as the plastic adheres to the cells

of the walls

of your lungs

it keeps you company

as you walk the streets

making your way to work

or to dinner after

it's not so much hope as intuition

something that you know directly

without needing to analyze it

it bridges the gap

between the unconscious and conscious

parts of your mind

a non-verbal certainty

that a time will come

when the residue of the human

will have disappeared

almost entirely

such that what is left of the world

will come to regard our time here

as a temporary illness

or weak parasite

that wasn't designed to kill

as much as seek out its own end in the host's body

I want you to hold this image in your mind—

a future that continues without us

is already on its way

having begun in the far distance

not as silence

but as a faint

nearly imperceptible noise

that emerges first as silence

then drowns out all other noises

a smothering nothingness

that expands

to take over the horizon

beyond which you cannot see

as it dips below your visual plane

as you sit here

listening to my voice

as we sit in the company of each other

and my voice and your thoughts become one

you begin to regard these words

what I am saying to you now

as amounting to nothing more

than clearing a place for us to rest

as we wait together

for the end of the world

for there's nothing to be done now

besides wait

building these little monuments to ourselves

along the way

say

a side altar to a forgotten saint

that no longer serves as a site of worship

it gives you a moment

to rest and kneel along its wood railing

light a candle or two

out of something like duty or habit

just something to do with your hands

briefly

before continuing on our way

but we know that there's nowhere left for us to go

that we've already arrived where we were headed—

this peripheral and inconsequential space

we've found

together

what we are building is simply this place of rest

as we wait for the true end of ourselves

and so

instead of grief

what we find is pleasure

instead of sadness

there's this feeling called heaven

that touches

however faintly

on happiness

one could say we're so happy

because our time here together is short

and we've prepared our own annihilation

now

all that's necessary is patience

all that's required of us

is to patiently wait for an end

we may never witness

except as the ripples of its effects

briefly visible at the edges of our time together

as though this feeling called heaven

were something like the waves of the ocean

gently lapping against the wet sand

as the tide slowly rises to meet

say

a blanket

spread out in the weak morning light

on which you're now calmly sitting

as you watch the day pass before you

your eyes unfocused among the grey waves

they crash near what seems like the edge of the ocean

and envisioning this kind of tranquility

projected out to a great distance

that only annihilation could promise

a pleasure almost too pure to experience

the final annunciation of the human in the world

spoken in a single voice

in the moments leading up to the moment before the last

in which some distant generation

lays down together

one last time

as you sit listening to my voice

I want you to think of this time to come

as a promise—

once our species' short timeline has reached its end

what is left will rebuild itself

our existence a scar

written across its surface

which in time will fade

as when your vessel or vehicle

records an error in physical movement

as it brushes against the unyielding world beyond it

forming an area of fibrous tissue

that replaces your once soft and supple skin

say

as you wash dishes for a friend and their partner

who were kind enough to let you stay with them

out of obligation

no matter how pleasant

that preserves the bond

built before your visit

that now only needs

this occasional maintenance

in the form of physical proximity

and so while they're out together

buying food for dinner

you want to do something nice for them

show them something you learned as a child—

that these minor gestures are what constitute a family

and you want them to know

even unconsciously

that you think of them as family

but when you place your hand

in an empty jar

the pressure from the rag and warm soapy water

causes it to break

and as the shards drop

from your hand to the sink

one cuts across the knuckle of your thumb

or pointer finger

so your blood

mixes with the pool of water

waiting to go down the drain

and out into the sewer

combining together and flowing beneath you

creating something like an abstract map

of your own movement

across the earth's surface

you come to regard these errors

as a catalogue of half-recalled embarrassments

that you hold onto in quiet moments like these

they reaffirm something you knew all along

but could never quite say

something about the body's poverty

for example

or its lack of grace

finally

for now

devoid of physical pain

that you could only bear witness to

in the vacancy of your own imagination—

the approach of this future world

emptied of our presence

is slow enough it could easily be confused with stillness

it is no longer a question of force

but of patience

for this end that seems always to be on its way

but never any closer

such that this feeling called heaven

discovered in this distant annihilation

might've seemed to remain forever on the horizon

if it weren't precisely that in this feeling

we're able to recognize attenuated pleasure

in the immediacy

of each other's presence

as you sit here

listening to my voice

I want you to remember that there's a pleasure

a small pleasure

but a pleasure nonetheless

born of the desire

to cultivate awareness

of how little time is left—

counting these minutes

or hours together

and in so doing

feeling time become corporeal

as we experience it

in the company of each other

one minute

followed by another

understanding each

as the second to the last

never more than we can handle

not yet

this feeling called heaven

or rather the acknowledgement

that annihilation offers a kind of pleasure

only recognizable

once finished

or complete—

therefore dissipates once it's become the center

of whatever little attention

it can garner

a pleasure that dissipates

not unlike fog

that dissolves as you wake in the morning

leaving a faint trace of condensation

visible off in the distance

it obscures your view

as you make your way to your car or the subway

or the bus

or whatever temporary and enclosed environment

carries you passively to your job

as you struggle to continue the difficult process

of waking up

again

this feeling called heaven

is a pleasure

only witnessed in the past tense

and from a distance

this sense of annihilation or future death

occurring now

a collective sense

of something having already happened

far off

while you were paying attention to something else

say

as you stand in the produce aisle of a grocery store

holding a sleeve of celery still wet from the overhead mister

and hear yourself

unthinkingly

singing along to whatever song is playing

over the store's PA

something vaguely recalled

but which for the brief moment of its singing

takes away the pain of

a loved one or family member's passing

which you thought to have stained even this chore

and as you stop

the words no longer leave your lips

your mouth closes of its own accord

shamed for finding refuge in something

as seemingly so inconsequential

as a pop song generic enough

to find its way into the background of your attention

you return to a conscious awareness

of your surroundings

the tiled floor beneath you

and the fluorescent lights above

as the environment returns

so too does the pain of their passing

the absence they created in your life

and as your attention returns

it brings with it an awareness

of your own grief

and its absence in that moment

a compacted nothingness

that seems to repeat itself

out and beyond this doubling

which increases in minute degrees of intensity

such that it pushes this pleasure

you barely knew you were in the process of experiencing

further beyond your cognitive grasp

until it's gone

I wanted to show you something

as an excuse to stay in your presence

or to put it as precisely as I can

to keep you here

in my presence

or each in the presence of each other

a little longer

with annihilation certain it is only

a question of love and this kind of minimal pleasure

I wanted to say something plainly

so that you would understand

I wanted to say something directly to you

to address you

as though I were holding your hand

or looking into your eyes

and saying something—

it feels like I'm lying here

next to you

my mouth close to your ear

whispering something

that you've felt but hadn't thought to say out loud

you didn't need to

because it's something you've understood

since before our time together

something you've known

without needing to put into words

it's not despite the destruction of the world

that you're worthy of love

but because of it

because you've helped to usher it in

through these minor acts of annihilation

and participation in this collective end

through what amounts to nothing

other than participation in your own life

this material expenditure

which is often so mindless

say

as you move through the aisles of a convenience store

picking up a granola bar or bottle of water

keeping your headphones in

to block out the noise of the store beyond

you swipe your credit card at the self-service kiosk

before exiting through the automatic doors

it's precisely that you can't help yourself

it's this inability to stop

that makes our own wordless sense of annihilation

in which we've come to understand

this feeling called heaven

as the most human thing we know

and therefore

the most deserving of love

yes

it's precisely in these moments

when you're at your most alone and isolated

lost in the slow expenditure

of the minimal energy necessary

to take part in your own life

it's when you move across the surface of a city

gliding from one job to the next

that you're most human

and therefore

the most lovable

or deserving of love

perhaps the real problem

is that extinction is taking too long

not that our own extinction

is unfurling before us

but that it's doing so

so slowly

that it almost seems

to disappear

so that the pleasure to be found in our own annihilation

this feeling called heaven

only recognizable in retrospect

once it's disappeared

replaced

not by a memory of pleasure

but the realization of having missed the chance

to make it a memory

or to put it another way

it's the sensation of having felt

this particular pleasure

after having felt it

unaware

whose remainder subsides—

a reverberating

and aching lack

that once it disappears

only exists as something that has gone

but gone without your ability to feel it go

it's this slow dissolve we missed

establishing itself

as the condition

upon which our world is built

as our backs were turned

to become this space at the end of the human

that we now occupy

together

we might've called it something different

like compulsion—

we're compelled to tell each other stories

in the same way

we're compelled to destroy the world

this end that unfurls

out before us is a story

poorly remembered and poorly told

cast into some inaccessible future

such that

all we have to say to each other

are these impoverished half-forgotten stories

but it's the pleasure of telling them to one another

recounting

and improvising

the lies and exaggerations

that in each other's company

make up a structure

a brief excursion on how nothing ends

except this ending which too

in time will meet its dissolution

or to believe

not in a future

but rather that the end is happening now

and yet we only are at its beginning

I wanted to begin by saying something directly to you

something like this is the end

have you say it back

so that in saying this

to each other

we could feel somewhere

in the back of our minds

below our conscious attention

and beyond this simple act of repetition

something else opening onto itself

say

the fact that one day

we'll look on days like these fondly

with an almost

imperceptible jealousy

that we ever had it so good

as though to say

there was a time

that we'd touch each other

when we didn't hurt

those who'll have come after us

might even call us fortunate to have been

in this place together

in each other's company

when the end had only just begun

when nothing had really changed yet

so that when we say something like this is the end

and embrace each other

I want you to remember

that what we're really saying

is that this is the beginning of the end

and as we speak softly to ourselves

in little more than a whisper

wanting to be overheard—

loved for the quietness

of the small part

we take in this collective murmur

loved as a small animal

at the end of a stranger's leash is loved

we recognize an absence of hope

as if hope were general

or a standard

against which to measure

whatever image we might have of a future

perhaps before we came together

you believed

in the continuance of this life

not of any one of us individually

but the undeniable fact of our survival as a species

you knew intellectually

we all die

some sooner than others

but death's guarantee makes this thought abstract

its concreteness absents any real sadness

instead

I want you to focus your mind

on denouncing the hope

embedded in the idea

of our momentum as a species

the belief that we will somehow continue

even after we've gone

or that somehow

someone

will be there to tell a story about us

to read out the names

inscribed on our graves

even if only to themselves

we've come to understand that what we are

now

is devoid of a future

that there's no future for us as a species

after a threshold

we can't see past

an invisible partition that allows us to continue

as we are

making families

going to work

participating in minor gestures of affection or distrust

cataloguing the grievances or joys

that come with living amongst each other—

it's not so much that we're doomed

but rather that we continuously acknowledge

that we've arranged this for ourselves

and more importantly

we made this arrangement

together

in a sense

it's the one time we've acted harmoniously

after killing however many countless others

throughout our time here

we've finally turned to ourselves

not with enthusiasm

but appropriate indifference

in organizing the world

around this feeling called heaven

we've come to realize

that we've arranged the world

such that we can't live on it forever

and in doing so

we've made ourselves temporary

but there's a freedom

in knowing we'll be able to walk away

from the responsibility

of living here

a freedom from the pain of being alive

granted to someone we'll never meet

the beginning of a time without pain

a collective fantasy of there being nothing

or a time when we could leave together

that makes something like

the desire for a final collective action

understandable

for it would be something we did together

whether out of hope for a better world

or a rejection of this one

because we understand now

that these are the same things

and that this time is different

this time the world is rejecting us

and in this rejection

there's an absence of the need of hope

as hope would acknowledge

even if unconsciously

that things should be otherwise

as if to say

we wanted something other than what we have

but this is all there is

there was never anything other than this

we wanted something different

to go on forever

even if it didn't include us

even if this forever didn't include us

it would finally become something

like harmony or agreement

just an end

a slow annihilation that already occurred in the distance

but has yet to arrive

its movement towards us a final promise

if there's any promise left it's this

or more accurately

more than a promise

it approaches us with slow certainty

before which everything's been stripped away

save the habit of continuing

the bare minimum of the human

stumbling through its little rituals

and consolations

advancing towards nothing

this beauty in the exhaustion of ourselves

as a species

this feeling called heaven

those who came before us

told us

that the world would end

they talked of redemption

but we've come to understand

that what lies ahead of us

isn't the redemption of the human

or the transformation of this vessel or vehicle

into some greater good

or some refined articulation

of what it means to be alive

but simply an end

if anything

the redemption of the human

is found in the slow ooze of the body

as it expires

unburied

on the ground

lying down

where it found itself

in that final moment

on its back

looking up at the sky one last time

as the clouds make their way

slowly

from the east to west

towards a shore

eaten away by waters that rise

beyond the daily fluctuations of their tides

as if walking into a clearing

instead of finding the remnants

of this wretched thing we call our body

this vessel or vehicle

we discover

that we never existed except as décor

a run-down building in need of repairs

beside a garden overgrown with weeds

the tools rusting in the ground

and the vegetables and fruit

unpicked

or fallen in the dirt and wet mud

as water pools around their roots

from the humidity that hangs in the air

anything but our bodies

rotting under the afternoon sun

finally liberated of the specificity of individuated death

all I wanted to show you all along was just

this feeling called heaven

this pleasure in knowing

that though we've poisoned the earth

it will continue without us

violence lessening

as it expresses itself

finally free of our guiding hand

the return to a balance

or quietness

we imagine existed before us

and as this violence is expressed

in progressively

more minor ways

as the center dissolves

imagine

what we would've once called atmosphere

I want you to remember

that this violence no longer has a subject

that the real utopia

our collective death

offers the world

is only found in our own dissolution

and as our violence continues without us

as a fact

needing no witnesses

it asks nothing of us

and yet

we can't separate ourselves from it

so this violence and our part in it are expressed

as waiting

or more accurately

a passivity that refuses participation

beyond the minimum effort of remaining present

for our end approaching far in the distance

aware that what we're waiting for

is simply us

come again

there's nothing left

but ruins yet to be made

we're simply that which has yet to fall apart

all that's necessary is to construct the altar

for the altar to disappear

a closing meditation

I'd like you to close your eyes

or lower your eyelids

to focus on the middle distance

of the floor in front of you

I want you to get comfortable in your seat

or if you're standing

stand with your legs slightly wider

than shoulder width apart

your feet firmly planted on the ground

and whether you're standing or sitting

you begin to feel a string

that starts at your seat

or the soles of your feet

and runs from your tailbone

up your spine

and out of your head up

to the ceiling above

as we begin

I want you to remember that all you are doing

is preparation for the journey ahead

and that you're safe here

and no one can hurt you

all you're doing is preparing for the journey ahead

and you're safe in the company of my voice

I want you to remember that violence is just information

or decorative like a video of lions and hyenas

fighting over the carcass of a wildebeest

or antelope

or some other dead animal

captured with night vision cameras

projected on the wall and playing

silently in the background

or if this proves too distracting

and takes away

from your ability to focus

on something other than the video

then visualize a still image projected on a sheet

that hangs in front of the wall

moving slightly in the air conditioner's breeze

a screencapped google image

of the sun reflecting off standing water

I want you to hold this image of the sun in your mind

and as you do

notice how it doesn't glitch

but moves in unison with the sheet

and in doing so

becomes not unlike "nature"—

both act as immersive backdrops or non-mediums

like the human voice

or my voice

speaking out loud to you now

describing or rather staging

a series of side altars

this bound method of procedure

my speaking to you now

produces an image like the reflection of the sun

or more accurately

a space for your thoughts to inhabit

as something to focus on

but only in the beginning

as my voice will prove more and more unnecessary

as it begins to disintegrate

into discrete regions of your mind

which you can visit for a time

or not

and leave as you will

and as I'm speaking to you

you'll begin to feel grounded

like you're resting comfortably on an empty platform

one that has been specifically prepared for you

but prepared poorly

or the platform itself is barely visible

the first plateau in an unexplored region of a video game

as you reach the clearing

it begins to rain slightly

a fine mist covers the air

now

as the water becomes general

and covers this wretched thing we call our body

this vessel or vehicle

the pain it experiences

even its pleasures

your twitching and convulsions

the spasms that involuntarily begin in the head

clouding your thoughts

and bringing them too much into focus

as the pain radiates out to your limbs

as you sit on this bare expanse

and the water begins to cover you

the pain and frustration

that sadness you first felt

alone on this plateau

stretching out to the horizon

these feelings start to wash away

and as they leave you

your mind becoming empty and relaxed

you can start to feel each individual drop of water

slowly trickle down your skin

joining the other drops

in their fall together to the plateau below

and feel the rivulets

descending down your left and right sides

they pool around you

creating a greater intensity of wetness

against your buttocks and thighs

as each drop

joins its mate and forms this community

this pool of cool and pleasant water

that washes away the pain and fear

you live with each day

you begin to sense the presence of those

who've gone on before you

as if in moving on

and shedding their vessels

they left behind a message written in water

that caresses your skin and soaks your clothing

so you can no longer tell the difference

between the rough cloth

and the flesh it covers

in this water

you sense the presence

of the anxieties they purged

from themselves

in moving on

giving up their bodies for a wholeness

not unlike the wholeness

you feel at times

when your own body disappears

in a moment of great joy or despair

and you are growing more and more aware of them

as you listen to my voice

and the wind begins to pick up

and the rain falls harder

as water lashes against this wretched thing

we call our body

until you feel the skin of your right forearm

begin to open

to form a canyon that faces the sky and the falling rain

but instead of feeling pain

you feel a sense of deep calm

the muscles in your right arm

your blood and tendons

open up to the bone

and greet the water

as it falls against your body

collecting in the space it made for itself

and as it does

your blood flows from the open cut

spreading across the water

watch it turn a faint purple color

growing paler and paler

until any distinction

between the blood from your vessel

and the rain disappears

as your blood ranges across the growing pool of water

you sense it mingling

with the presence of those gone on before you

alone on this plateau

you sense their presence

and are assured with the fullness of their company

as the water rises up your thighs

covering you to your belly button

and as the water continues to rise

it covers the plateau

an infinity pool

stretching out to the light grey sky turning blue

without a decrease in the rain

that no longer falls but seems to swell of its own accord

moving and caressing your body

as the water reaches your chest and neck

it's as though the clothes you once wore

have been stripped away

and are no longer necessary

and as the water covers you

instead of feeling buoyant you feel grounded

instead of rising to the surface

you stay firmly seated on the plateau

an anchor in your mind

or something that hovers just below

the surface of your thoughts

rooting you to this world

and the vehicle of your body

as the water rises over your head

reaching up to the same colored sky

both a light blue and turning slightly

as if in a clean glass bowl on an empty wooden table

mirroring the movement of the larger room around it

feel your body now

sitting beneath the surface of this cool clear liquid

and open your mouth to speak or breathe

to call out to those who've gone on before you

remember that this is the time you've prepared for

and that you're ready

remember your plans

you try to take a breath you can't

until you stop trying

and step out of this earthly vessel

like stepping through a door into another room

only then can you rise up to the surface

to find that your body has gone

and your soul become infinitely small

floating like a microbead of plastic

riding the undulating surface of the water

under a cloudless and crystal-clear blue sky

and lost in clarity of this color

you begin to return to the room

and as you do

I want you to hold in your mind

this image of microbeads

floating together

a buoyant plastic fog spread across the water

an image of something you sensed all along—

you are perfect

and this journey you've prepared

stepping away from the plateau

into the surrounding waters

requires no faith nor leader

no father nor mother

no system

beyond the lives we are already living

this material action

our bright faces and warm smiles

as we greet each other in the morning

or say goodnight before bed

the very fact of our existence extends out

towards our own extinction

as a pod of dolphins

arching their backs

and moving their flukes

vertically

up and down

to generate momentum in the neon blue water

propel themselves forward

and out of the waves

and back again

framed by purple flames

and the chants of those who came before

singing with one voice

in the background

Thanks to the editors of *A Perfect Vacuum* and *Social Text* where sections of this book were first published. Thanks to Gauss PDF, who released a video of the coda entitled *a first meditation.*

I want to thank Kim Calder and Evan Kleekamp for their support and care, as well as Lindsey Boldt for her insight throughout this process. Thank you to all my friends and family; especially, Bruce Algozin, Brandon Brown, Alejandro Crawford, Gordon Faylor, Rob Fiterman, Lewis Freedman, Trisha Low, Mark Johnson, Poupeh Missaghi, Bridget Talone, Aaron Winslow, and Steve Zultanski for reading and commenting on drafts of this book; deepest gratitude for Chris Sylvester, Marie Buck, Shiv Kotecha, and Diana Hamilton—my plague family.

Finally, this book is for Holly Melgard to burn for warmth once I'm gone.

Joey Yearous-Algozin is the author of *Utopia*, and the multi-volume *The Lazarus Project*, among others. With Holly Melgard, he has co-authored a trilogy of books *Holly Melgard's Friends and Family*, *White Trash*, and *Liquidation*. He is a founding member of the publishing collective, Troll Thread. He lives in Brooklyn, NY.

NIGHTBOAT BOOKS

Nightboat Books, a nonprofit organization, seeks to develop audiences for writers whose work resists convention and transcends boundaries. We publish books rich with poignancy, intelligence, and risk. Please visit nightboat. org to learn about our titles and how you can support our future publications.

The following individuals have supported the publication of this book. We thank them for their generosity and commitment to the mission of Nightboat Books:

Kazim Ali
Anonymous
Jean C. Ballantyne
Photios Giovanis
Amanda Greenberger
Elizabeth Motika
Benjamin Taylor
Peter Waldor
Jerrie Whitfield & Richard Motika

In addition, this book has been made possible, in part, by grants from the New York City Department of Cultural Affairs in partnership with the City Council and the New York State Council on the Arts Literature Program.